# TILLEY TRAVEL TIPS

## FOR SAFE, EASY, WORRY-FREE TRAVELLING

by
## ALISON TILLEY

**Cartoons
by
GRAHAM HARROP**

Published in 1994 by: Alison Tilley Productions


For more information contact:
Alison Tilley
900 Don Mills Road
Don Mills, Ontario
Canada M3C 1V6
**(416) 441-6141**

**Dedicated to my father, Alex Tilley —
a wonderful man whose love, support and
encouragement continues to inspire me.**

His company, Tilley Endurables, makes the
best travel and adventure clothing
*— and quite possibly the best catalogue*
— in the world. If you call 1-800-ENDURES,
I'm sure you'll be sent one free.

**Canadian Cataloguing in Publication Data**

Tilley, Alison, 1969 -
Tilley travel tips for safe, easy, worry-free travelling

ISBN 0-9697771-2-4

G151.T55 1994    910'-2'02    C94-932036-6

1. Travel - Handbooks, manuals, etc. I. Harrop. Graham.
II. Title.

# CONTENTS

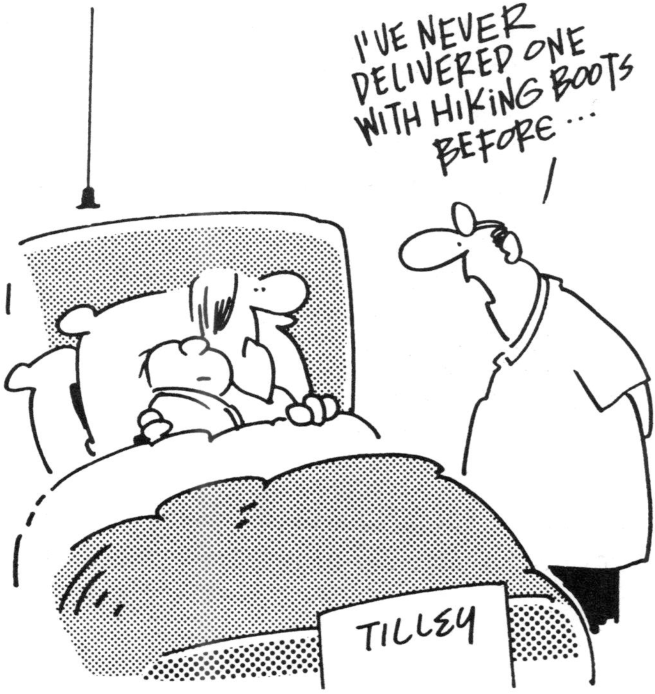
I'VE NEVER DELIVERED ONE WITH HIKING BOOTS BEFORE...
TILLEY

# INTRODUCTION

## WHY THIS BOOK?

As early as I can recall, I've been fascinated with exotic places. Travelling was a big part of my family life when I was growing up, and we went every year to places like Guatemala and Belize, which were relatively untouristed then. There's no doubt my parents helped spark my curiosity and relentless desire to explore.

When I started travelling on my own at the age of 16, I had no idea how to organize a trip. The only thing I knew about travelling was that I wanted to do a lot of it. I set out for a summer in Europe with three suitcases and a duffle bag that were so heavy in total (about 45 kilograms/100 pounds) that I couldn't carry them all at once.

Since that first overburdened solo trip nine years ago, I've been around the world twice and have learned a lot about successful travel, especially about the importance of travelling lightly. I wrote this book because I want to share the insights and information I've gained.

In my travels, I've been lucky to experience what I once only dreamed of doing. I have gone trekking in the Himalayas with Sir Edmund Hillary, swum with dolphins in Australia, climbed an active volcano in Indonesia (and had my breakfast cooked in it!) and spent months backpacking, and hitching rides on sailboats in the South Pacific islands.

I'm a dreamer who listens to my dreams. There are a lot of heavens on this Earth and it's become my mission to discover them. For me, travelling is inspiring, empowering, fascinating — and it gives me a breather in the whirlwind of everyday life. It has nourished my spirit and made me more self-reliant, aware and appreciative. It's definitely the best thing I've ever done for myself.

If you're a would-be wanderer who longs to travel, be it for a week, a month or a year, I hope this book will help you to realize your dreams.

Alison Tilley

# 1 FIRST THINGS FIRST

☐ Make sure your passport is valid for a reasonably long period of time, even if you're planning to visit for just a few days. Many countries require that a passport have at least six months' validity left.

☐ Your travel agent and airline will know if the country you're visiting requires a visa — a stamp in your passport permitting you to enter that country for a specified period. They can also tell you where to get it, and whether you can get it upon arrival or need it in advance. Allow four to six weeks if you're getting one in advance. It's preferable, if possible, to get your visa before leaving home, since some countries will hold your passport if you apply for a visa from outside your country of residence.

☐ Carry extra passport-size photographs in case you need to get a visa en route. (I take six with me for a year-long trip.)

☐ Check with your local public health office at least 10 weeks before departure to find out which inoculations you need and where the nearest travel inoculation clinic is.

☐ If you plan to drive abroad, get an International Driving Permit from your local automobile association. They're valid for one year and cost about $5.

- 13 -

ANSWERING MACHINE MESSAGES
BURGLARS LOVE MOST..

# 2 KEEPING YOUR HOME SAFE

☐ Use automatic timers that turn lights and radios on and off, to give your home an occupied appearance. (The electricity to run a small radio for one week costs about $4.)

☐ Ask your insurance agent about home checks while your home is unoccupied. You may not be covered if your home has not been visited while you're away on vacation.

☐ Have a neighbour or friend collect your mail or, for about $3 a week, have it held at the post office.

☐ Stop newspaper delivery.

STILL THINK IT WAS A WASTE OF MONEY TO HAVE THE LAWN MOWED WHILE WE WERE AWAY...?

☐ Arrange to have your lawn mowed or snow shovelled.

☐ Be sure the message on your answering machine does not imply that your house is vacant.

☐ Have a neighbour park his or her car in your driveway.

☐ About 80% of the stolen property recovered by the police cannot be identified and returned, so it's sold at public auction. To make sure you can identify your property, use an electric engraving pencil, which police will loan you, and inscribe your driver's licence or social insurance number on valuables.

# 3 WHAT IF I'M SICK?

Sometimes we North Americans take our health care system for granted and assume that similar treatment and services are available free-of-charge worldwide.

Unfortunately, this isn't always the case. My father says, "Prepare for the worst to happen, and smile when it doesn't." On the ninth day of our trek in Nepal at an altitude of more than 16,000 feet, he slipped and badly pulled a muscle in his leg. Unable to walk, he was evacuated by a military helicopter, which cost him about $1,000 US because he had no insurance to cover this kind of emergency.

☐ Shop around for the supplementary health insurance that best suits you. Try travel agencies, automobile associations and student travel services. Your gold or premium credit card may even provide travellers' health insurance as a perk.

☐ Always carry your insurance policy and provincial health card with you when travelling. You may need them to be admitted to hospital.

☐ I recommend becoming a member of the International Association for Medical Assistance to Travellers (IAMAT). You'll receive a comprehensive booklet listing English-speaking doctors in 120 countries around the world. These doctors have all had some training in North America or Britain, are familiar with North American medical standards and practices, and charge set fees to members: $45 US for an office visit, $55 for a hotel visit, and $65 for an evening or weekend appointment. Membership also includes a world immunization chart, listing the shots you'll need for various countries and giving information on malaria, which is more widespread than you'd think. Although there's no membership fee, donations are appreciated.

Write to IAMAT at 40 Regal Rd., Guelph, Ont. N1K 1B5; phone (519) 836-0102. In the United States, write to 417 Center St., Lewiston, N.Y. 14092; phone (716) 754-4883.

☐ **Don't Drink the Water**, edited by Dr. J.S. Keystone, is a 100-page comprehensive manual that provides commonsense, up-to-date health advice for international travellers. Written in an easily readable and entertaining style by travel medical experts from across Canada, it costs $14.95 plus $2.50 postage and handling. Write Health Resources Centre, Canadian Public Health Association, 400-1565 Carling Ave., Ottawa, Ont. K1Z 8R1; phone (613) 725-3769.

## TO KEEP HEALTHY...

☐ Avoid drinking tap water (including ice cubes) unless you're sure of its source. Bottled water is safest. (I drink three 1.5 litre bottles a day). Beer and soft drinks are also worry-free. Keep a bottle of water in your bathroom to brush your teeth with.

☐ Eat at well-known and busy restaurants that look clean and well run.

☐ Remember to use sun block with an SPF rating of 15 or more and apply it to all exposed skin — including your ears and tops of your feet. Wear a hat and closely woven clothing.

☐ In tropical or wilderness locations, check your shoes before putting them on, as a precaution against scorpions and other nasties. It's a good idea to shake your clothes too, just to be on the safe side.

MAKE SURE YOU SHAKE OUT YOUR SHOES BEFORE YOU PUT THEM ON...

☐ Your best prevention against being bitten by mosquitoes, which carry malaria in some countries, is to:

☐ Wear a loose long-sleeved shirt, long pants and socks.

☐ Use an insect repellent with high levels of Deet.

☐ Avoid wearing perfume, scented deodorants or fragrant hair products.

☐ Sleep under a mosquito net and a ceiling fan.

☐ If you take medication, bring enough to last the whole trip, plus some extra in case of delay. Also, bring the generic name in case you need to buy more.

☐ Split medication into two containers and keep one in your carry-on luggage, in case you lose the other. If you carry a syringe with you (for diabetes or allergies), it's wise to have an official letter from a doctor to avoid problems at customs inspections.

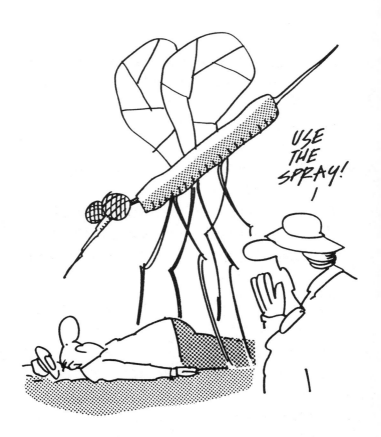

# 4

# SERVICES FOR SAVVY SENIORS

I became friends with Lennart in Tonga, a group of islands in the South Pacific. He's a 76-year-old adventurer who taught me that wanderlust doesn't lessen with age. Here are some organizations and books that older travellers will find helpful.

☐ **The Canadian Association for Retired People (CARP)** publishes a newsletter for its 100,000 members, informing them about a wide variety of discounts for car rentals and hotels. Open to those 50 and older, membership costs $10 a year or $25 for three years. Write 27 Queen St. E., Suite 1304, Toronto, Ont. M5C 2M6; phone (416) 363-8748.

☐ **The American Association of Retired Persons (AARP)** offers a wide range of benefits to people over 50: motoring plans, health and car insurance and a magazine called *Modern Maturity*. Membership is $8 US a year or $20 for 3 years. Write P.O. Box 199, Long Beach, California 90848; phone (202) 434-2277. Within the U.S., phone 1-800-441-2277.

☐ The **Canadian Bureau for International Education** publishes *What in the World is Going On?*, a helpful 210-page book for Canadians only, that includes information on more than 300 work, study and volunteer programs. The book costs $16 plus $3 postage, and can be ordered from 220 Laurier Ave. W., Suite 1100, Ottawa, Ont. K1P 5Z9; phone (613) 237-4820.

# 5 ACCESS TO THE WORLD

☐ The Health Sciences Information Centre of the Jewish Rehabilitation Hospital has one of Canada's most comprehensive collections of information for travellers who are physically disabled: 880 pamphlets provide information on access to historical sites, accommodation, restaurants, museums and transportation in North America, Europe, the Caribbean, Australia and other places. Write 3205 Place Alton Goldbloom, Laval, Que. H7V 1R2; phone (514) 688-9550.

☐ The Travelin' Talk Network is an organization of 1,000 disabled people who network with each other by phone, providing all kinds of information about their hometowns. Their 550-page directory ($35 us) lists all members and includes information about where you can find accessible transportation services, hotels with open bed frames and much more. To join the network, subscribe to their eight-page quarterly newsletter or order the directory, write P.O. Box 3534, Clarksville, Tennessee 37043; phone (615) 552-6670.

☐ **Handi-Travel: A Resource Book for Disabled and Elderly Travellers** provides lots of practical tips and useful resources. Published by the Canadian Rehabilitation Council for the Disabled, it costs $12.95 plus $3 postage.

Author Cinnie Noble was appointed to the Order of Canada for her outstanding efforts in making travel more accessible to people with disabilities. Write 45 Sheppard Ave. E., Suite 801, Toronto, Ont. M2N 5W9; phone (416) 250-7490.

# 6 WEN-DO MAKES WOMEN'S WAY SAFER

One of the best things I've ever done was to take the Wen-Do Women's Self-Defence course. In just 15 hours I learned practical, easy-to-remember, physical, verbal and mental techniques to protect myself. It's amazing how much safer I feel since taking the course.

Wen-Do (which means "women's way" in Chinese) is suitable for all females 12 years and older and can be learned in either two day-long sessions or a series of evening sessions. In my class, a 72-year-old woman took the course with her grand-

daughter and loved it. Wen-Do also offers courses for women whose mobility and hearing are impaired, and their trainers will fly almost anywhere to teach it. The course cost $60 and I highly recommend it. For more information, write P.O. Box 139, 260 Adelaide St. E., Toronto, Ont. M5A 1N0; phone (416) 533-1202.

# 7 HOW TO RUIN A PICKPOCKET'S DAY

☐ The most important possessions you need to protect are your passport, travellers' cheques, money, credit cards and airline tickets. Carry these items with you at all times or keep them in a secure place like a Tilley secret pocket, a money belt or a hotel safe.

☐ Avoid advertising your wealth. Keep expensive cameras hidden in a small day-pack and leave costly jewellery and watches at home.

☐ Remain alert to what's happening around you. Be aware of loud arguments, bumps and other incidents, which may be staged to distract you while someone else lifts your wallet or handbag. Buses, train stations, airports, outdoor festivals, subways and other crowded places are popular with pickpockets.

# 8 CHOOSING THE RIGHT ROOM

Whether I'm checking into a youth hostel, guest house or hotel, I always ask to see three different rooms so I can choose and compare. For safety's sake, I also ask for a room on an upper floor, near an elevator, (not near stairwells, which thieves use for an easy escape route).

In each room, I look at the view, check the door and window locks (and air conditioner, if there is one) to make sure they work, pull back the bed covers to see if sheets are fresh, flush the toilet, turn on the shower to make sure it runs and listen to the traffic noise. (The higher the room, the quieter.) The entire process takes only a few minutes and helps me get the best room wherever I go.

QUIT COMPLAINING! HOW OFTEN DO YOU GET A FREE ELEPHANT WITH SIX GLASSES...?

# 9 A SHATTERING EXPERIENCE

My sixteenth birthday present from my dad was airfare to Europe for my first solo trip. On the second day of my holiday, with great eagerness, I bought six gorgeous, heavy, green drinking glasses in Amsterdam as a thank-you gift for my dad, not thinking at all of the fragile weight I was adding to my load.

I struggled my way around Holland, France, Italy, Greece and Spain for two months, lugging three over-packed suitcases, a large duffle bag and a heavy purse. My gear was so heavy I couldn't lift all of it at the same time! When I finally returned home (with the glasses intact), I proudly gift-wrapped them and presented them to my dad. Wouldn't you know, that very evening, he accidentally smashed one of the glasses!

The lessons I learned were threefold:

☐ Over-packing can seriously ruin a trip. Travel light and you'll travel happy!

☐ Suitcases and duffle bags are not practical if you'll be moving about a lot. Your arms can only carry so much weight before feeling strained, which is why backpacks are so practical.

☐ Remember, whatever you buy, you've got to carry with you or else ship home.

# 10 GET THE RIGHT GEAR

I've tried duffle bags, backpacks, suit-cases and combination backpack/suitcases and found that a combination backpack works best for my kind of travel, which is long-term and low-cost. My backpack works three ways: it's a backpack; it's a shoulder bag; and it's a suitcase. The shoulder straps zip inside the pack when they're not needed (during airline flights), and it has a shoulder strap and a handle in the middle. These combination backpacks look more like a big bag than a backpack, hold a lot, and are much easier to carry

than a duffle bag, suitcase or hard luggage. When you carry one, you have the added advantage that your hands are free! Get a good-quality one with internal metal frames and ask an experienced salesperson to mould the frame to fit your back.

☐ If you prefer a large suitcase, consider one with sturdy wheels that are replaceable (they may wear down) and that pivot for turns in elevators. Or use a portable folding carry cart.

☐ Zippered side pockets provide useful extra space, but don't put anything valuable in them since they're obvious targets for light-fingered folks.

☐ A hand-strap or leash is practical for pulling a wheeled suitcase, but when you check your baggage at the airline counter, remove the leash so it doesn't get caught and damaged on a conveyor belt.

# 11 PACKING POINTERS

☐ Eliminate any item that has only one use unless it's essential. Be ruthless. If I don't think I'll wear an item at least twice a week, it stays at home. It's far better to have too little than too much. And remember that you can usually buy whatever you need overseas, unless it's Tilley clothing — and that, you wear on the plane!

☐ Take only what you can carry yourself. The ideal is one bag that fits under your airplane seat. Add a backpack and you can travel the world!

☐ Pack those items you dare not lose (medication, toiletries, camera, etc.) in your carry-on bag in case your luggage goes astray.

☐ Pack toiletries and cosmetics in plastic (never glass) and put them into a sealable plastic bag.

☐ Select a basic shoe that's suitable for both day and evening wear.

☐ I use recycled plastic bags to pack: beachwear in one, T-shirts and shorts in another, warm clothing in another and an extra bag for laundry.

☐ Pack shoes in a breathable cloth bag. Baking soda in exercise shoes helps control odour.

# 12 GETTING OUT THE WRINKLES

☐ Put rolled socks in the necks of shirts, blouses and Tilley Hats to help them keep their shape.

☐ If you're having clothes dry-cleaned beforehand, ask the cleaners to fold them so they're ready to pop into your case.

☐ Layer clothing by putting waistbands of pants and skirts at the hinge edge of your suitcase, and letting the leg or skirt hang over the far edge. To avoid sharp creases, place soft items such as sweaters on top, and then fold pants or skirts over them. Smooth out all wrinkles after each layer.

☐ You can also use tissue paper or plastic dry-cleaning bags between layers to prevent creasing. Plastic bags are best because they trap air, which acts as a cushion.

☐ Hang any travel-creased clothing in the bathroom while you shower; the steam helps to remove the wrinkles. If your rumpled clothes are Tilley Endurables, sprinkle them heavily with water, then hang to dry. They dry swiftly.

For backpacks, it's often best to roll clothes to avoid wrinkles. Place pants, for instance, on a flat surface, lay other lightweight items on top and roll up as you would a sleeping bag.

# 13 LIGHTEN YOUR LOAD

The secret to keeping it light is to include just the right stuff. My pack weighs only about 12 kilograms (26 pounds), even when I'm going away for 10 months. I've learned to leave out a lot since the days when I travelled with three suitcases! Here's what I include for warm-weather adventures:

- ☐ A Tilley hat
- ☐ Long shorts and drawstring shorts
- ☐ Tilley cotton 6-button shirt and 3 short-sleeve cotton shirts
- ☐ Comfortable sandals that look good with everything (I think Mephistos are best).
- ☐ Water-repellent hooded windbreaker
- ☐ Running shoes
- ☐ Thongs for shower and beach
- ☐ Camera, case, film and lens cleaner
- ☐ 2 bathing suits
- ☐ Good-quality sunglasses, neck cord, case and cleaning cloth
- ☐ Beach bag
- ☐ Mask and snorkel
- ☐ A sarong: I pack a colourful piece of lightweight cotton (roughly 3 feet by 6 feet). This handmade sarong makes an excellent beach towel, skirt and cover-up and can even be used as a sheet on warm nights.

WE REMEMBERED TO BRING THE FIRST-AID KIT, THE SUN BLOCK, TRAVEL ALARM, SMALL FLASHLIGHT AND INSECT REPELLENT AND THEN WE LEFT THE SUITCASES IN THE TAXI...

- [ ] Sunblock with an SPF of at least 15
- [ ] Travel alarm clock
- [ ] Small flashlight
- [ ] First-aid kit
- [ ] Socks and underwear
- [ ] Bug repellent and mosquito net (for countries where malaria is prevalent)
- [ ] Biodegradable laundry soap and disposable wet tissues
- [ ] Pens, paper, small notebook
- [ ] Recording Walkman, three blank tapes and six (no more) of my favourite tapes
- [ ] A couple of good reading books
- [ ] A few pictures of family, friends and significant pets to help with the occasional bouts of loneliness
- [ ] A *Lonely Planet* guide book for each country. I highly recommend *Lonely Planet* travel guides. Having purchased 18 of them in the past nine years, I have found that they've saved me enormous amounts of money, time

and energy. They're perfect for all ages and budgets and cover virtually every accessible part of the world. With the detailed help of *Lonely Planet* guide books, I've travelled alone around the world comfortably, safely and confidently. Through them I've discovered my favourite countries, which are (in order of preference): Indonesia, Fiji, New Zealand, Nepal, Australia and Guatemala.

## CLOTHES FOR COMFORT AND SECURITY!

☐ My father is recognized as the designer and maker of some of the best travel clothing in the world. Tilley Endurables are good-looking, long-lasting and comfortable. They have secret pockets, security pockets, and "give 'em hell !"

washing instructions. Tilley Hats are so unique that strangers who wear them often stop and chat with each other, especially in foreign lands! The catalogue is probably one of the best you'll ever read. Phone 1-800-387-0110; in Toronto, 444-4465. Within the U.S., phone 1-800-338-2797.

☐ **TRY TILLEY ENDURABLES TRAVEL ADVISORY SERVICE**
All it takes is a phone call and Tilleys will send you a two-to-four- page information package on the country you plan to visit. You'll learn about entry requirements, dos and don'ts, holidays and weather information for the dates you intend to be there. Phone 1-800-387-0110 in Canada. Within the U.S., phone 1-800-338-2797. There is a $3 charge.

CAN YOU BELIEVE THIS...?
- THEY WON'T LET YOU
INTO ANY EUROPEAN COUNTRY
UNLESS YOU'RE
WEARING TILLEY
ENDURABLES...!
TILLEY
ADVISORY

# 14 PACKING TIPS

☐ Your clothes often indicate the level of respect you show for the cultures you're visiting. Jeans are often inappropriate. The more your body is covered, the better dressed you're generally thought to be.

☐ Remember that in tropical climates, most buildings are air-conditioned and you may need a sweater or shawl for indoor wear.

☐ Look for lightweight, easy-to-care-for, hand-washable clothing. Test each item for comfort by sitting, squatting and kneeling while wearing it.

☐ Consider the customs of the country you're visiting. In a Muslim country, for example, you're not allowed to enter a mosque with bare shoulders. In many places, short shorts are frowned upon. In remote villages in the mountains of Nepal, it's appropriate to cover most of your body. Women often find culottes or skirts suitable attire just about everywhere, and long shorts are frequently suitable when short shorts aren't.

☐ Never take new shoes on a trip.

☐ When purchasing hiking boots, buy at least half a size too big. This prevents black-and-blue toenails when going down steep hills.

☐ Bring a small sewing kit with thread that matches your travel wardrobe.

☐ A pocket calculator is handy for converting foreign currency.

☐ Outside of North America, hotels don't automatically provide toilet paper, a face cloth, a sink stopper, face soap or bath towel: so pack your own.

☐ Bring a small day-pack made out of a sturdy fabric. (Thieves can slash lightweight ones).

☐ Pack 2 toothbrushes (in case you lose one) and dental floss.

# 15 BAGGAGE TIPS

Although less than 1% of checked baggage goes astray, it's annoying when it happens. Here's what you can do to help ensure that yours doesn't.

☐ Remove all old destination tags.

☐ Attach a tag inside your luggage, and outside, with your name, address and phone number.

☐ Make sure the check-in agent puts a correctly coded destination tag on every one of your bags. (Every destination is assigned a three-letter code.)

The last time I caught the wrong code on my destination tag was in Thailand, where my pack was accidentally tagged to go to Malaysia instead of Indonesia!

☐ Use an unusual luggage tag or co-loured ribbon to help you identify your luggage quickly on the carousel. I hand-painted the outside of my back-pack with brilliant blue-green water-proof paint and love it!

☐ Select luggage with combination locks, or buy a small padlock for your backpack and lock the zippers shut. Have your partner carry a spare key or, if you're travelling solo, tuck the spare into your money belt or Tilley secret pocket.

☐ If you're concerned that your baggage may not make the connection flight, ask the ticket counter agent for "door storage," which means your bags will be last on and first off.

AMERICAN EXPRESS
WE CAN ONLY REPLACE YOUR TRAVELLER'S CHEQUES IF YOU LOSE THEM FIRST...

# 16 MONEY MATTERS

☐ Carry your money with you at all times, but not all in the same pocket or money belt.

☐ Write down the serial numbers of your travellers' cheques and keep the list in a different place from your cheques. Always check in advance about the refund policy for lost or stolen cheques.

☐ Take 20% more money than you think you'll need.

☐ Carry a combination of travellers' cheques, cash and credit cards.

☐ Bring $40 US in one-dollar bills for tips and cab fares.

☐ Start out with a small amount of cash (the equivalent of $50) in the currency of the country you'll be visiting. This should be enough for taxis, tips or small necessities on arrival, before you get to a bank or exchange booth with your travellers' cheques.

☐ Take a moment to estimate how much you should pay or receive before any foreign transaction. When changing travellers' cheques, watch the teller count the money in front of you, then count it back carefully in front of him or her.

## GIVE YOURSELF CREDIT

- ☐ Take two widely used credit cards such as American Express and Visa.
- ☐ Make sure your cards won't expire while you're away.
- ☐ Before you go, get the fax number of your bank and the manager's name. Then, if you need more money while abroad, fax them to send you a draft. Specify the city you're in, the bank and its exact address. (There could be a dozen branches of a bank in one city.)
- ☐ Bring some personal cheques along, otherwise you'll have trouble buying travellers' cheques or getting a cash advance.

## CHANGING TRAVELLERS' CHEQUES

- ☐ Expect to pay a 1% charge to cash travellers' cheques at exchange offices. A bank or credit card company often won't charge you. The poorest exchange rates are often given at borders, railway and airport exchange offices and hotels and restaurants.

☐ Buy most of your travellers' cheques in denominations of hundreds and fifties, with about $200 in twenties and tens. Toward the end of your journey, you may want to change a small cheque to get you through the last day or so.

☐ Be prepared to present your passport when cashing travellers' cheques abroad. (Be sure to put it back immediately into your security pocket or money belt.)

☐ In out-of-the-way places, American dollars are the most easily exchanged and accepted. American Express travellers' cheques, with their instant replacement policy, have made my travels much easier and I won't leave home without them.

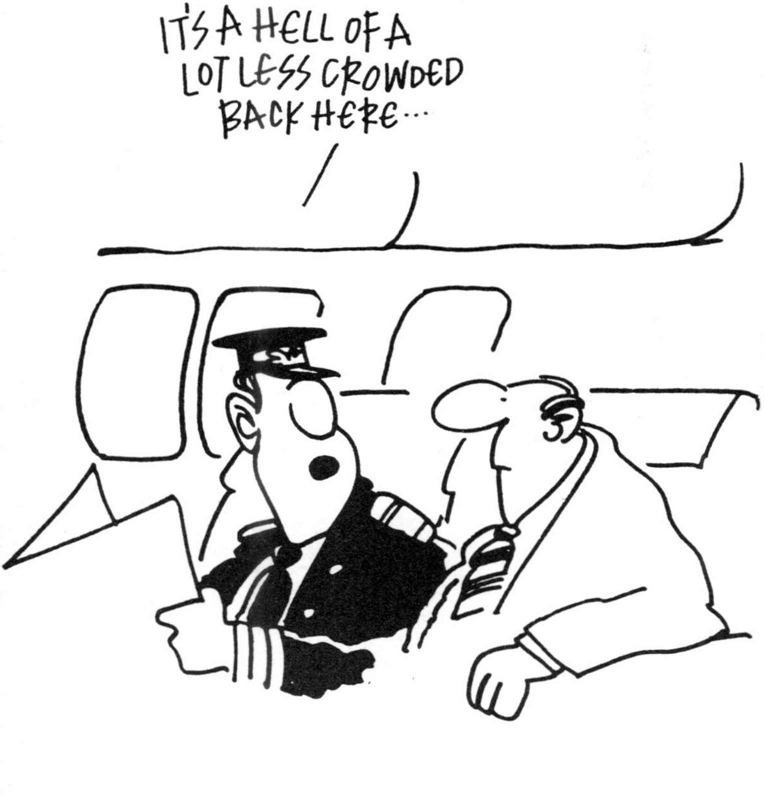
IT'S A HELL OF A LOT LESS CROWDED BACK HERE...

# 17 FLYING TIPS

To make flying more pleasant:

☐ Ask to sit in the front row or beside the emergency exit if you have long legs.

COMFORTABLE...?

- ☐ Drink plenty of water or juice every half hour or so to prevent that Sahara-Desert-like feel in your nose, throat and eyes.
- ☐ Bring eye drops and remove your contact lenses in flight. (The dry cabin air may cause sore eyes.)
- ☐ If you fly all night and aren't able to get any sleep, try to avoid going to bed when you land as it only prolongs your adjustment to the new time zone. Try to stay awake until it's bedtime in your new surroundings.
- ☐ Wear loose clothing with an expandable waistband since your body may swell during a flight.
- ☐ Bring a jacket or sweater since cabin air temperatures may fluctuate.
- ☐ For long flights, ask for a window seat so you can lean against it and sleep.
- ☐ Avoid alcohol and caffeine, as they cause dehydration and can disrupt your sleep pattern.

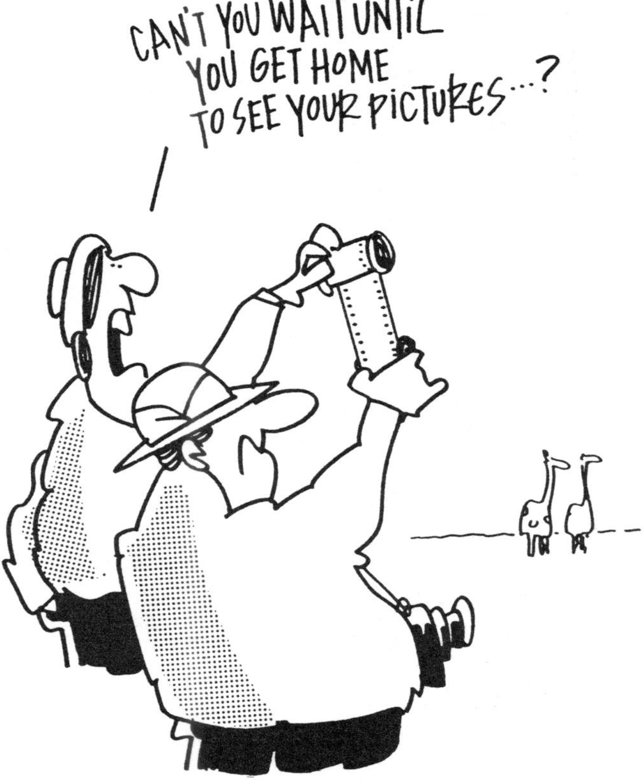
CAN'T YOU WAIT UNTIL YOU GET HOME TO SEE YOUR PICTURES...?

# 18 FOR PHOTO BUFFS

☐ Bring lots of film with you. It can be very expensive abroad so pack more than you think you'll need.

☐ Develop your film at home. Development chemicals differ in other countries and results are often less than satisfactory.

☐ Ask, with at least a smile or gesture, before taking a stranger's photograph, since camera customs vary in each country. You may offend someone in a Muslim country or land yourself in prison in a country with a military dictatorship.

☐ Tape your business card to the inside of your camera case and to your camera. (There are millions of honest souls in the world.)

☐ Consider bringing along a Polaroid camera, as my father did in Guatemala. When he gave people photos of themselves, it usually gave him unlimited rights to click away with his 35 mm camera, and made for lots of smiles.

☐ Take photos in the early morning or late afternoon for best light conditions.

☐ To avoid facial shadows and give more punch to pictures, use a flash nearly all the time when photographing people.

☐ Get the names and addresses of people you've captured on film and mail copies of photos to them. (They'll be delighted!)

☐ Try to include yourself in as many pictures as possible. It's often more interesting to have people in photos instead of just scenery. You'll appreciate it later.

- 96 -

# 19 KEEPING THE PHONE FARES DOWN

☐ To avoid hotel surcharges, which can be enormous, call from a post office or phone office (there's usually no surcharge), and use your telephone calling card (surcharges will be minimal) or call collect.

☐ If you know you'll be making phone calls home from overseas, a no-charge service called Canada Direct provides travellers with special access numbers for 65 countries, which put you through directly to a Canadian phone operator. For a free brochure and a wallet-size list of the numbers, call 1-800-561-8868. Calls are billed at Canadian operator-assisted overseas rates, which tend to be cheaper, and you won't have to wait as long for your calls to be connected.

# 20 TELLING TALES

I find it much easier to speak for an hour than to write letters. If you're like me, consider taking a recording Walkman on your trip to capture your thoughts, impressions and memories. I've sent dozens of what I call "talk tapes" home to my family over the years and find it such a warm, comforting way to keep in touch. A 90-minute talk to someone you love can cost less than $6 to mail, which is considerably cheaper than a telephone call. By the way, regular-size cassettes are more widely available around the world than mini ones.

In addition to sending talk tapes home, I've been recording my private journal on cassettes since I was 13 years old. I now have over 100 private talk tapes — and I think they're a great gift to pass on to kids and grandchildren.

# 21 LIFE ON THE OCEAN BLUE

If you've got time on your hands and adventure in your heart, consider crewing on a yacht. Whether you're looking for a day jaunt or a six-week trip from California to French Polynesia, sailors around the world are generally happy to take on crew.

In Tonga, I spent four days sailing and island hopping with a delightful couple from San Diego. In Perth, Australia, my mom and I spent an exhilarating evening as guests in a two-hour sunset race on the Indian Ocean.

It's easy to organize and no experience is necessary for crewing — just a desire to lend a hand with general maintenance or cooking. Call a few yacht clubs to find out when races are scheduled or when the busiest times are. Arrive at the club 90 minutes before a race begins, approach a few people, tell them where you're from and simply ask if you can join them.

You'll probably be welcomed with open arms. (Bring along some cheese and crackers to share.)

For those wanting to sail on longer trips:

☐ Read the classified ads in sailing magazines or place one yourself. I put up notices at marinas and yacht clubs in the South Pacific and was able to go on a lot of day trips as a result.

☐ Choose a boat that will give you at least 10 feet (3 metres) of length per person to allow for some personal space.

☐ Go for a short trial trip to see if you enjoy each other's company.

☐ It's customary to share food costs: $50 US a week per person for food is standard.

# 22 MAKING THE WORLD BETTER

☐ If you've always dreamed of mapping a volcano, tracking whales or discovering dinosaur bones, here's your chance. The nonprofit organization Earthwatch finds paying volunteers to help scientists on research expeditions in 58 countries around the world. You can spend two to three weeks as an Earth Corps volunteer. For a free copy of their magazine or to join, write 680 Mt. Auburn St., Box 403, Watertown, Massachusetts 02272; phone (617) 926-8200.

Sometimes in your travels, you'll see malnutrition, disease and poverty that make you realize how fortunate North Americans are. That's how Doreen Wicks came to found Global Ed-Med Supplies (GEMS), a Canadian organization that helps to educate people in developing countries at a very grassroots level in health issues, education and becoming self-sufficient. To inquire about GEMS, write 77 Harbour Square, Suite 3201, Toronto M5J 2S2; phone (416) 923-6865.

# I'D LOVE TO HEAR YOUR TRAVEL TIPS

If you have a travel tip you'd like to share, please send it to me. I'd like to include them in future publications.

Alison Tilley
c/o Tilley Endurables
900 Don Mills Rd.
Don Mills, Ont.
M3C 1V6